WHY ME

ALICE LEONARD WALKER

Order this book online at www.trafford.com
or email orders@trafford.com

Most Trafford titles are also available at major online book retailers.

Print information available on the last page.

ISBN: 978-1-4907-9598-0 (sc)
ISBN: 978-1-4907-9597-3 (hc)
ISBN: 978-1-4907-9599-7 (e)

Library of Congress Control Number: 2019909037

Trafford rev. 09/17/2019

Trafford
PUBLISHING® www.trafford.com

North America & international
toll-free: 1 888 232 4444 (USA & Canada)
fax: 812 355 4082

ACKNOWLEDGEMENTS

To my supportive Daughter Keishanda Moseley, who see after her mother every day and my Devoted Husband Hayward Walker who always take care of his wife.

Thank you God for my Husband.

CONTENTS

CHAPTER 1

IN THE BEGINNING

Looking back over my life coming from an abusive home, I remember my dad abused my mother. After a night of drinking, he would come, pull her out of bed, and start beating her. She was meek and humble. She wouldn't even fight back.

My sister, Emma, asked her, "Why wouldn't you defend yourself?"

When Dad came home, the atmosphere changed. It put fear in all of us. My brothers

tried to stop him, and he would give them a good whooping. My sister, Emma, said that she had made up in her mind that when she got older, she would do something to turn things around. He would work and take care of us, but he loved to drink. Every time he would go out with his friends, he would come home very intoxicated. He was also unfaithful to my mom. He even went out and had a child with another woman. I remember he would always bring me a little surprise when he came in from work.

After nights of abusing my mother, she would try to hide her hurt, but we knew what was going on. The only thing my mother would do was stay home, cook, clean, and take good care of us. My sister had made up her mind that when she was older, she would confront him for what he did to our mom, but she did not believe in revenge. My brothers would try to

help my mother when he would abuse her. But he would start whipping them and made them go back to bed.

Mom would say, "Go back to bed. It will be all right."

This continued every weekend when he went out drinking. Our mother would always have his meals ready when he came home from work. This continued for years. But when you do wrong, it will catch up to you. My mom did not want us to have on our conscience that we hurt our dad.

She would say, "God will fix it."

One cold rainy night, our dad was out with his friends drinking. That night, he did not come home. Early the next morning, it was still raining. My baby brother cried all night long. Mom never went to sleep. The next morning, I was standing on the porch, the rain fell from

the house top into my hands when I looked up and saw a car approaching our house. They were in a hurry, and I realized it was my mom's sister and her husband. They ran to tell my mom the news.

She got up from her chair, rushed to the door, and said, "Something is wrong."

Before they got to the porch, my mother asked what was wrong.

Her sister said, "We have bad news about your husband."

CHAPTER 2

BAD NEWS

She said, "Robert was killed last night in an auto accident. He fell out of the truck and broke his neck. And it killed him instantly."

Mom began to weep, called us all together, and said, "I will have to be the daddy and mother, too. Your dad was killed last night."

But my mom did not accept how he had died. She did not tell anyone after the funeral.

She told us, "I don't believe it happened that way. I'm going to ask God to show me in a dream what really happened."

Sometime later, Mom had a dream about the accident. They were going down a hill. It was raining. She did not get all of it, but they opened the door and pushed him out, and they never went back to check on him. Mom told us who did it but not to say anything. That has been one of our secrets.

My brothers wanted to kill that person, but Mom said, "No, no. God will take care of it."

So we slowly watched this person wither down to nothing, and he soon died of cancer. He suffered much before he died. He could never look our mother in the eye again. He never knew that we knew what he had done. My brothers tried to catch him by himself, but

God did not let it happen. Thank God! We let it go because Mom had hurt enough.

After Dad's funeral, we were sad, but we were happy for Mom. She did not work, but she soon had a job and took good care of us—six children, two girls and four boys. It was not easy for Mom. When the eldest boy grew up, he tried to help Mom with the rest of us. And he did a great job.

CHAPTER 3

A WONDERFUL MOTHER

After Dad's death, I remember our school teacher came to talk with Mom. When our teacher finished talking, Mom had a job in the school's cafeteria preparing our meals at school. She was the best cook. When she finished cooking, she walked one mile to get home so she could have our evening meal ready and our clothes washed and ironed; but,

we still had our chores to do. The boys had to cut wood and stack it inside. The girls had to do the dishes, clean the house, and help wash and iron clothes.

Every weekend Mom would bake what we called tea cakes. They were delicious. We had a back door, and Mom would put the tea cakes in a huge bowl and leave it sitting on the kitchen counter. It would be filled with tea cakes. We would sneak in the back door, get one, and split it. After a while, we would hear our mom call one of our names.

She would say, "Come here. Who stole a tea cake?"

There would only be one missing, but she could tell. We wondered as there were many cookies how she knew one was missing. We wondered how she could tell. That was a mom who knew her children. One child would blame

another one, and if we did not tell the truth, we would all get a whipping. But we still loved our mom because we knew that Mom would do without if she thought we were hungry. However, always had plenty.

When my brothers grew up, they tried to bring some money in to help. Mom appreciated that. When the boys all graduated, left, and got married, they brought money back to help out. Then our sister, Emma, finished high school, went to college, and made it as a nurse. She made us all proud. Then one of our brothers graduated, left home, got married, and was working for the City of Dallas. He and our sister were a big help to the family. Finally, my other brother graduated and went into the Navy, but Mom worried a little about him.

Then I graduated, went to college for nursing, and worked at St. Paul Hospital

for a period. I left and went to work for Texas Instruments. Then I married Leroy Moseley, a wonderful man of God. We tried unsuccessfully to have a baby for sixteen years. Twelve doctors in Dallas said it was medically impossible for me to get pregnant.

CHAPTER 4

MY MIRACLE

The Friendly Memorial Baptist Church pastored by Rev. A. W. Bullock was where I received the Lord, got involved with the Word, and later received the sacrament of baptism of the Holy Spirit. Jesus came into my life, and I have never left Him since, and I know He will never leave me. My husband and I were faithful to His Word.

Then my pastor delivered a message: "All Things Are Possible If You Can Believe."

I told my husband, "The man of God said God can do anything if you can believe, so let's believe."

I had an issue with my blood. I had told no one. Later I was on my knees in my bedroom praying to God to heal me and give us a baby. I heard a knock at my door. I only wanted to talk to God. I knew if anyone could help me, it would be Him.

I heard the Holy Spirit say, "Answer the door," and I did.

It was my pastor and his wife. They saw the tears in my eyes and told me the Lord had sent them. I began to tell them what I had been going through for twelve years. They asked me if I believed that God could heal.

Then my pastor said, "Sister, if you don't have the faith, my wife and I will have it for you."

At that time, I had not known how to use my faith. They put me in a circle. Then they began to pray for my healing.

Shortly after they ended the prayer, he said, "Sister, God is going to heal you today, not tomorrow."

Then I was so happy, and he said in one year, there would be three in the family. I thought, "Can this be true? Because the doctors said it was medically impossible." But what I had not known at the time was that God is a healer if we can believe. It was 10:00 a.m., and by 4:00 p.m., my body had been healed.

In one year, I was two months pregnant with my daughter. That was my miracle, and I was in church. I had not yet received the sacrament of baptism, but later, I did receive the Holy Spirit.

I have been with the Lord ever since, and I never want to leave Him because I know He

will never leave me. He is in my life forever, and He is the best thing that could have ever happened to me. See, God can do what man can't do. Just trust Him, and He will be right on time. He protected my household even when I was a little girl, when the enemy had tried to take me out as a child. But I had made it only because of the grace of God.

Just before I became pregnant, tragedy hit us again.

CHAPTER 5

TRAGEDY HITS ONCE AGAIN

Our mother became ill and had treatments for cancer, but it just kept getting worse. Then the doctors transferred her to M.D. Anderson Hospital. She just kept getting worse. Our sister took over and was with our mother every day. We lived in Dallas. We, the family, personally thanked our sister for a job well done.

When my sister made the last call to me, saying I had better come, I was at work. I left work, got on the plane, and told my supervisor I did not know how long I would be gone. He assured me that whenever I returned I would still have my job. When I got to where Mom was, she was getting worse by the minute. But the Lord had already spoken to me and said she would not be with us on Christmas. Sure enough, she left us before Thanksgiving. When the Lord spoke to me for a few seconds, I could not breathe.

Then I said, "Okay. If you are ready to take her, then I am ready to give her back to you."

In two days, she was gone. We grieved and moved on. It was not easy, but God, for one more time, brought us through. A few months after, I found out I was two months pregnant

with my daughter. She was born early but had few problems. She is a beautiful young lady.

My daughter and I had another tragedy. Her dad became ill, entered the hospital, and started getting sicker. We were already divorced, and he had remarried. Then he was placed on a ventilator. In the operating room, he caught an airborne germ. It attached itself to his brain. Then he became brain-dead. They told us we should take him off the ventilator, but it was not my call because we were divorced, and my daughter and her brother did not want to make that choice. So his brother had to have the life support removed. Then the Lord brought us through.

In 1999, I lost my daughter's father, four brothers, and the last uncle. Each death was two weeks apart. Everyone thought I was going

to have a nervous breakdown, but I told them I was okay because Jesus had me. I had to help choose a casket for most of them and help make funeral arrangements; but again, God brought me through.

When we live in this world, we have to go through some things, and whatever they are, please don't let them make you bitter. They will teach you that life has its ups and downs. They will help you change your perspective so that you will realize that life is about choices. You can choose to become better, or you can choose to become bitter. It's up to us to take the bitter with the sweet and turn everything into *lemonade*. You can have a pity party and feel sorry for yourself or read this book, and *it will guide you to the light* waiting for you at the end of the tunnel. Then the darkness of depression and despair will

disappear. Your life will become exciting and adventurous. Take it from someone who has been through many trials and tribulations. God delivers us out of them all. God will carry you through.

CHAPTER 6

GOD IS A HEALER

My daughter had gone through something when she was born. She weighed two pounds. She could not come home until she weighed five pounds. That was a long time to be away from my baby whom I had waited on for sixteen years. Her valves had not developed completely because she came at seven months. She would have to sleep with her mattress standing straight up. If not, she would suffocate if no one was there. I had to

stay in the house with her for three months. No one was to be around her but her dad and me because if she caught a germ, she would become very sick. Oh, I prayed so heartily, and she was very healthy. She had never been sick to the point that she had to go to the doctor except each year to get a checkup. Thank God! She was a very healthy eater. She was small but very healthy. I had to hold her upright every time she ate until her valves developed.

I went through a lot with her, but it has been worth every bit of it. She grew to become very intelligent, and most of all, she received God at the age of eight. She can explain the Book of Revelation in the Bible better than I can. She witnessed to two young ladies when she was led by the Spirit. She sees things before they happen—the same as her mom. She married a wonderful young man who is a deacon in the

church. Now she does not have any of those problems with which she was born. And she takes good care of her mother daily. She eats all-natural food.

In 1999, I lost my daughter's dad and four brothers; but again, God showed His glory on me. I went through four years of sickness from 2012 to 2016.

But I remembered what our mother told my sister and me, "You must go through to get to."

Now I know without a doubt that my work for God has just started. It is my season because I know without a doubt that I have been gracefully broken. Remember, all who read this book. Remember that life is a choice.

CHAPTER 7

GOD'S GRACE IS SUFFICIENT

I am now married to a wonderful man named Hayward Walker, whom I respect; and he respects me completely. My daughter loves him because of the way he treats her mom.

Then suddenly, he became ill. They ran tests, and they said he had bone cancer—another trial. We went through so many changes. The

doctors wanted him to let them rearrange his whole body. He asked me what he should do because they told him he had a year and a half to live. I told him no one could make that decision except him, so he thought about. He called me in the room one day, and said that he had made the decision not do that procedure. He would wait on the Lord. A friend, Gloria Haggerty, came over and prayed for him and told him it was left up to him as many others were praying also. He kept undergoing treatments for a while.

Then all of a sudden, he said, "I am tired of going to the doctor every week," and he quit going.

He started doing better and better. Like Gloria had said, he had accepted that he was healed. Like she had told him, God had healed him. Where the doctors had given him

a year and a half, God has given him almost ten years. How does He do it? Glory to God! He had a choice to make. Thank God he had made the right choice. Thank God he had lots of prayers. God's grace is sufficient.

CHAPTER 8

PRAYER IS POWERFUL

When the anointed prayers reached heaven, Jesus was moved. Thank God also that He made the right choice. The Lord sent one of His prophets to my house early one morning. Before I had become ill, I told her, whatever the doctors said, just to say, "Alice is going to be all right."

He carried me through the valley of the shadow of death. I did not know why He wanted me to repeat that, and every day for a week I said the Lord's Prayer. If you have ever experienced going through the valley of the shadow of death, then you know what it's like. It is scary going through there.

You have to know Jesus said, "Speak it and believe."

I had no doubt because I knew He had sent to me a true prophet, Gloria Haggerty. I obeyed, and I'm still here. If I had not obeyed, I would not have made it. All I can say is if you know Him, trust Him. In all your ways, acknowledge Him, and He will direct your path. See, we go through things sometimes not just for ourselves but also so that we can help others.

CHAPTER 9

FAITH IS ACTION

In 2012, I became very ill and went to the hospital. They ran all kinds of tests on me, and they knew I was very ill, but the tests did not show any illness.

They said, "We will have to send you home because we can't find anything."

They were saying that I wasn't going to make it much longer because I had congestive heart failure.

I was so sick, and I asked them, "How could I have come in here two days ago with a good heart and now you tell me I've got congestive heart failure?"

I told them that I did not believe that. They discharged me. I came home and did not tell my husband what they had said. They sent me home because they did not know how much time I had.

I said, "Lord, you said Alice is going to be all right."

I could not tell my family because they would begin making funeral arrangements, and I knew what God told me to say in spite of what the doctors had said.

I told my husband the next morning, "Take me to Presbyterian Hospital."

He said, "Okay."

The next morning, we made it to Baylor. The doctor had me sit on the examining table, while listening to my side, my back, and my chest.

He said, "Mrs. Walker, you have pneumonia."

I knew I did not have congestive heart failure. They kept me for two days and sent me home. I recovered at home.

If you are ever in doubt, trust Jesus. I promise if you believe, He will see you through. All things are possible if you can just believe and not doubt. I came home knowing God had said I was going to be all right, and I was because He is not a liar. Have faith in God.

CHAPTER 10

A NARROW ESCAPE

I was out helping an elderly person. It was hot. She looked at me and asked if I was okay. I said yes.

She said, "You don't look okay. Let your daughter drive you to the emergency room."

She got out and walked home, and I started feeling a little strange. All of a sudden, I started talking funny and could not pronounce my words. My mouth moved to the side near my ear. It frightened her. I was telling her to drive.

By then, I knew I was threatening to have a stroke. I began to pray in English.

Then I heard the Holy Spirit say, "Pray in the heavenly language."

I did, and by the time I arrived at emergency, it was gone; but I told them I was threatening to have a stroke.

They looked at my face and said, "Well, we don't see any sign of a stroke."

I said, "Maybe not now," but I was threatening to have one.

They rushed me to the back, started running tests, and said I had two TIAs (Transient Ischemic Attacks), which were threats of a stroke. God had saved me from that. I knew He would do it. I just trusted Him, so that was a narrow escape. God did it for me.

CHAPTER 11

GOD'S GRACE IS SUFFICIENT

When we can't trust anything or anybody, God's grace is enough, anytime, anywhere. I am a living witness. If you are reading this book, you should know by now that it is only by the grace of God that I'm still here, enclosed in my right mind, leaning and depending on Jesus. Prayer is powerful. Just

pray. Let Him know how much you love Him, appreciate Him, and trust Him for all your needs, and I promise He will see you through it all. Prayer is powerful. Do that every day.

CHAPTER 12

HE BROUGHT US OUT

The Lord brought us through—not that we've been so good. It's because He is good. I'm getting ready to open a business called: lifestyle changes that can make a difference in your life. If it had not been for the Lord, we never would have made it. We did not bring ourselves out. He did, and I am glad about it.

Thank God my family and I chose not to be bitter because of what we have gone through. We could not help what our dad did, but we can make a difference with the choices we make for our children. We have our hands to hold one another and work to help one another and our mouths to encourage and lift one another up. Remember, ask God to help you make the right choices. *God bless.*

CHAPTER 13

OBEY HIM

Always remember His Word says obedience is better than sacrifice. No matter what it seems like to you, just obey Him because if you don't, you will pay a price. Sometimes it may not look so easy, but He will not tell you to do anything you cannot do. Just like He will not put any more on you than you can bear. Believe me, He knows how much we can stand. The reason we say we can't do some things He tells us to do is because the

flesh is weak, but He is strong. So He will never allow you to go into any situation alone.

I know sometimes we ask, "Why me?" But when you come into an understanding that you are a child of the King, then you will say, "Why not me?" Sometimes God has to break us to make us see the purpose to which we are called. That's why He was bruised for our iniquities, and by His stripes, we are healed.

That's why His Word says, "In all thy getting, get a good understanding."

One Sunday morning, while I was in the service at Friendly Memorial, I heard the Lord say, "It is time for you to move on." My heart seemed to drop because I had been there for twenty-eight years. And He said, "If you don't, there will be consequences."

When I left that Sunday, I never returned as a member. The Lord told me to go back the

next day to make sure my name was cleared to leave.

When I called my pastor and asked him to meet me at the church, the Lord clearly spoke to me and said, "This is the scripture he is going to use because he does not want you to leave."

Sure enough, when I told him the Lord said it was time for me to move on, he said, "Sister, the Lord gave you to me."

He quoted the scripture to me that the Lord told me he would use. And this was what I had asked my pastor: "Is there anything that I have done to you or anyone that I should ask you or them to forgive me of? Have I done anything to any of the members within the church?"

He immediately said to me, "Sister, you don't bother anyone. Go in peace and stay with the Lord, wherever He sends you."

Then I left with tears flowing. You see, I saw God work in him so many times. When he prayed, God healed people right then and there. His life was threatened so many times. He would go to Mississippi and hold revivals until his brothers called him and told him not to come back to Mississippi for a revival because they were planning to kill him.

We were so afraid for him, but he said, "I am not afraid."

When he preached at other churches, he would have a prayer line so long, it extended out the doors of the church and down the street. It was something to see. I witnessed it so many times. When he prayed for me, God healed me. This issue that I had with my blood for twelve years, the Lord revealed it to him. He prayed. God healed me that day.

CHAPTER 14

THIS IS WHAT FAITH CAN DO

Others prayed, but I was not healed. When He sent me to Pastor Bullock's church, he and his wife prayed for me and told me if I did not have faith, they had faith, and they prayed.

He said, "God is going to heal you today, not tomorrow."

That was ten o'clock in the morning. By four o'clock that evening, I was totally healed and have been healed ever since.

I asked God, "Lord, you showed others my sickness. They prayed, but I still was not healed. Why?"

The Lord said, "You must use faith, along with clean hands and a pure heart."

I am so glad that I know Him for myself. You can't make me doubt Him because I know too much about Him.

When I came home the last Sunday from that church, I sat in my living room, and I said, "God, I know you don't want me to sit at home when you said it was time for me to move on."

I did not hear the Lord say anything. Then that Friday, I was driving down Buckner Boulevard in Dallas, Texas.

And the Spirit said, "Look to your right."

And I did. I saw this church.

The Lord said, "I want you in that church Sunday."

So I obeyed, but between Friday and Sunday, the Lord put me in the Spirit and showed me the inside of the church, the color of the carpet, where the pastor's study was, and showed me this man standing in the doorway.

I asked God, "Are you telling me this is going to be my new pastor?"

He showed me the place in the church where I would be sitting. When I got there and was seated, the Lord said, "Look where you are seated," and it was the same place he had shown me in the Spirit. It is so amazing to see things before they happen.

When the pastor came out, he had the same robe on that God had shown me in the

Spirit. I left after the church service was over, and Pastor Smith stopped me at the door and invited me to come back. I told him I would, and I went back the second Sunday.

At the time the invitation to the church was given, I asked God, "Lord, you want me to unite, or you want me to keep visiting other churches until you tell me where you want me to be?"

God immediately said, "I don't have to send you from church to church to know where I want you to be."

And without hesitation, I united with the Ebenezer Memorial Missionary Baptist Church, with Rev. A. D. Smith as the pastor.

CHAPTER 15

ANOTHER TEST OF MY FAITH

I was at the Ebenezer Memorial Missionary Baplist Church, where the pastor was Rev. A. D. Smith. I really did like the services and enjoyed serving there. Then after five years, sickness came. That was a trial because the Lord took me somewhere He had never taken me before. I kept getting sick. I was in and out of the hospital. They did not know what was

wrong when God sent His messenger, Gloria Haggerty, to me before I became ill. She told me the Lord wanted me to repeat the Lord's Prayer every day for five days and then take communion for five days. I had no idea why He wanted me to do that, but I obeyed.

She also said, "He said whatever the doctors say, just say, 'Alice is going to be all right.'"

Then within three weeks, I was in the hospital. They could not find out what was wrong. They sent me home and told me they did not know how much time I had.

Then I said, "Lord, you said Alice was going to be all right."

Then I became so ill. They put me back in the hospital. They said I had congestive heart failure.

I told them, "How could I have come in here with a good heart two days ago and now I've got congestive heart failure?"

But I could not let my faith waver because God said Alice was going to be all right. They sent me home again. I was right back the next week. I was transferred to intensive care. They found out that I had pneumonia, and at that time, people were really dying from that sickness. They gave me the wrong medication twice. When I called the desk, there were no nurses to be found. I stumbled to the desk, almost passing out, no one in sight.

I said again, "Lord, you said Alice was going to be all right."

When I finally made it back to my room, I called downstairs, and they called code blue and my room number. I said to myself, *Why are they calling code blue and my room number?* I

managed to sit up in bed. I was waiting when they came through the door. I told them to get away from me. They looked at me so strangely. So I was okay, and they left.

Thank God for my pastor, Reverend Smith, and the entire congregation for their prayers. You all really took care of me during that time. My husband and daughter really appreciate what you have all done for me. You will not go unrewarded by Jesus. I want to give a special high five to Ella and Clara at our church. They checked on me every day and made sure I had everything I needed, which they do for everyone. That means our pastor has taught them to see after the sick. I have really been blessed since I've been there. I love my church and everyone there.

You see, I have experienced much since I've been there, not talking about the time

that fear was so strong on me, it tried to take me out of here. I told no one but my husband and daughter. Through it all, I want everyone to know that I mean Jesus all the way. You see, the Lord told me this was my season. I have been tried. I've told all of you one of my secrets. The rest, I will take to my grave. But I want you all to know I've been through the valley of the shadow of death and I made it. Now I must be about my Father's business because I have been *gracefully* broken by God. I have changed my talk. Instead of saying, "Why me?" I can say, "Why not me?"

Wish me well on my Christian journey since I now know my gift and my calling. Peace be still with you.

CHAPTER 16

TO MY PASTOR AND OUR FIRST LADY

Pastor Smith, I could not close this book without thanking you and Sister Smith for a job well done. You gave me the Word, whether I liked it or not. You always keep your hands in God's hands. *Thank you!*

Sister Evelyn Smith (First Lady), you are one of the best first ladies. I admire your patience and your smile. When you hurt, you hide it

well. When you sing, your voice is so anointed. You sound like an angel.

To the Ebenezer congregation, you all know I love every one of you. I'm so glad God sent me your way. I give to you thanks and love that you may not have understood, but it was *real* and true.

CHAPTER 17

YOUR BODY

At four o'clock in the morning, I was awakened by the Holy Spirit, and the song that came so strongly into my spirit was "Gracefully Broken." Pay attention to your dreams. God sometimes speaks to us in dreams. But all dreams are not from God. Remember, whatever you go through, you are not alone. Whenever we have a need, He will never work a miracle off what you need but off what you've got. Our bodies are the

temple of God, so be careful what you do with it and what you put in it. Don't try to change it. Just take care of it, and it will take care of you. We are all in this world together to *love one another*, not to abuse one another with our hands and our mouths.

CPSIA information can be obtained
at www.ICGtesting.com
Printed in the USA
FSHW010224021019
62545FS

9 781490 795980